Be
BEAUTIFUL
Be YOU

Be
BEAUTIFUL
Be YOU

LIZZIE VELASQUEZ

Liguori
LIGUORI, MISSOURI

Imprimi Potest
Harry Grile, CSsR, Provincial
Denver Province, The Redemptorists

Published by Liguori Publications
Liguori, Missouri 63057

To order, call 800-325-9521
www.liguori.org

Library of Congress Cataloging-in-Publication Data
Velasquez, Lizzie.
 Be beautiful, be you / Lizzie Velasquez.
    p. cm.
pISBN: 978-0-7648-2079-3
eISBN: 978-0-7648-6747-7
 1. Beauty, Personal. 2. Spirituality. I. Title.
 RA778.V433 2012
 613--dc23
                         2012024865

Liguori Publications, a nonprofit corporation, is an apostolate of The Redemptorists. To learn more about The Redemptorists, visit Redemptorists.com.

Printed in the United States of America
17 16 15 14 13 / 6 5 4 3 2
First Edition

*I dedicate this book with love
to my brother and sister,
who support me through thick and thin
and who, with my parents,
are my biggest cheerleaders.*

*Thank you for everything
you have done for me.*

Love,

Lizzie

Contents

Foreword

When Lizzie asked me to write the foreword for *Be Beautiful, Be You*, I was immediately taken back to my younger years, when I felt that first sting of criticism—the kind that creates a deep enough wound that even at age thirty-seven, residual emotions occasionally rear their heads.

We all have days when we don't feel pretty enough, skinny enough, or worse yet—good enough. We need to break this pattern of unattainable aesthetic stereotypes that have intellectual and psychological repercussions. It's a societal issue that has gotten out of hand, and Lizzie has the courage to do something about it.

Lizzie's story is remarkable: Lizzie has a rare condition that doesn't allow her to gain weight, and her birth was a miracle in itself. But the more poignant marvel is the way she's managed to continually take hit after hit and still wake up every day putting one foot in front of the other.

Imagine being gawked at and whispered about every time you step out in public. I admire Lizzie for her determination to hold her head high in a world that places so much emphasis on outer beauty.

If you take only one thing from Lizzie's story and advice, I hope it's the idea that no matter what your current circumstance, change is possible. You are the master of your domain. You create your future.

We're all victims of something, but that's not who we are. What defines our character is the way we react to our situation.

I salute Lizzie Velasquez for being the warrior of light we need when it comes to understanding that all dreams are achievable.

Cynthia Lee
Anchor/Reporter, Fox 29, San Antonio
Publisher and coauthor, Lizzie Beautiful

Introduction

I have been given an amazing life. It hasn't always been easy, and it sure hasn't been predictable. Some people might say, "Hey Lizzie, you're only twenty-three, how can you be ready to write a book about your life?" My answer is to smile, nod, and think about my journey.

A lot has happened in these last twenty-three years, and I can truthfully tell you that I wouldn't change a thing.

Writing this book has given me the opportunity to look back at the events that have brought me to where I am today. Some still bring tears to my eyes. I hurt for the little girl who just wanted to be liked. And the YouTube video experience was very painful to write about.

Memories brought on other memories, bad and good. I remembered each challenge and success and all the good times I've had with my friends and my family. I've been blessed with both.

I prayed for all of you as I worked on this project. My goal wasn't simply to write a book, see my name on the cover, and feel good about the accomplishment. My goal was to share my story in a way that would allow me to connect with each of you and show you how to make your life better.

I also wanted to tell you that talking to God has given me the courage to keep moving forward. I'm not telling you that God will give you everything your heart desires or that your life will be easier or harder than mine. I'm telling you God has a plan for you and that he will walk beside you every day. All you have to do is talk to him and listen to him. God shows us how to live—if we let him.

God loves us faithfully. He loves me and he loves you just as we are, today, right now, right here, no matter where we are or what's going on in our lives. God listens to our words and hears the quiet whispers in our hearts. Each of us is given the opportunity to have a unique relationship with God.

Is someone or something hurting you? Are you feeling alone or lonely? Afraid? Misunderstood? Do you wish even just one person would listen to you? Do you have a decision to make and need help choosing a path? I want to give you the tools to figure out what to do about each of those problems.

God has given me an amazing life. God has also given *you* an amazing life. I care about you. God cares about you. I want you to understand that *knowing God makes the difference.*

I hope you find a lot to smile about on your journey.

CHAPTER ONE

Hi, My Name Is Lizzie

For surely I know the plans I have for you, says the Lord,
plans for your welfare and not for harm,
to give you a future with hope.
Jeremiah 29:11

ey, Lizzie, Mrs. Velasquez. It's almost show time!" CNN producer Dan Sterchele gave a welcoming smile from the doorway before disappearing back down the hall. After weeks of anticipation and planning, we were finally inside the huge CNN building in downtown Los Angeles. This was actually happening—and I was determined to enjoy every moment of it.

One day earlier I had been home in Austin, Texas, with my parents, and now Mom and I were sitting in the hair-and-makeup room getting ready for my next big TV interview. I closed my eyes and said a quick prayer asking God to be with me during the interview and to please calm my mom's nerves. She's always nervous enough for both of us when we do interviews.

Seconds later, my eyes flew open. The bright lights around the giant mirrors reminded me of a backstage dressing room on a Hollywood movie set. I watched as makeup-artist Aubrey airbrushed my face with the perfect shade of foundation. Since I'm blind in one eye and have only limited vision in the other, putting on makeup can be difficult, and I'm always worried about leaving the house looking like a clown. Aubrey was wonderful about answering my questions and giving me tips on how to put on the right amount of makeup without overdoing it.

My mother was being pampered in the chair next to mine. She looked like she was finally relaxing.

Minutes later and looking gorgeous, Mom and I were escorted back to the green room, where Dan was waiting to do the pre-interview questions. We sat on the long blue couch, and he told me to pretend we were on the set.

I took a deep breath, said OK, and sat up straight, ready to turn on my interview skills. We went through the questions one by one, often stopping to laugh at my answers.

"Definitely make sure you say that—that's really good!" Dan would suggest.

Minutes later, he said someone would be in to put microphones on Mom and me. As soon as he left, I jumped up. It was time to check my appearance.

Just like the one in the makeup room, the mirror in the green room (which, by the way, was light blue) had big, bright bulbs all around it to give off the perfect amount of movie-star lighting. I walked right up to it to get a closer look at my hair and makeup, and I loved them even more.

My dark skinny jeans were good to go. My deep-orange blouse

was just right, although I was a little worried because it was sleeveless, and studios are usually freezing. But at least I'd look cute! My long gold-circle necklace went perfectly with my big brown dangle earrings.

I'm not all that into shoes like pretty much every other girl my age is. Give me a pair of ballerina flats or boots, and I'm happy. But today I had on a new pair of cute brown leather boots. Since my legs are very thin, it's almost impossible to find boots that fit and aren't way too big at the top. Luckily, I had found a pair of size-two boots in the kids' department that were a perfect fit.

A man came into the room, clipped a tiny microphone to the front of my shirt, and did the usual count-to-ten test of the volume. I've worn microphones like this a hundred times, but this time there was something new. He gave me an earpiece—the exact earpiece I've seen singers wear during performances. Cool!

"OK, Lizzie, it's showtime!" I glanced at Mom as my heart started racing. I still wasn't nervous—it was more like I was about to take off on a crazy, fun, rollercoaster ride.

We walked down the hallway and stopped in front of a regular-looking door, but when Dan opened it, on the other side was another world.

The set was awesome. Giant cameras and headset-wearing men were ready and waiting. I stood at the entrance for a moment, looking at the brightly lit mini-stage. It was designed to look like a living room, with a coffee table, two smaller chairs grouped together, and one chair on the far left.

Mom and I were led to our seats. As soon as we sat down, Mom reached for my hand. I could feel my excitement soar as I scanned the room. The bright lights, cameras, teleprompters, and producers were only a few feet away, but my mind was already focused on the show.

"Lizzie?" With a welcoming smile, host Dr. Drew Pinsky shook my hand, then mom's. Like many people, I've been a fan of Dr. Drew's for a long time, and having the chance to meet him and be on his show was a dream come true.

I took a deep breath and gathered my thoughts as the producer counted down. Five, four, three, two. Instead of saying one, he pointed to Dr. Drew, and it was action.

We were on the air, and I was ready to tell my story.

My name is Lizzie Velasquez, and I'm twenty-three years old. I study communications at Texas State University. I adore small dogs, listening to music, hanging out with my friends, shopping for clothes, going to the movies with my family, and just being lazy. I'm also a reality-show junkie.

I'm a lot like any girl my age, but I'm also different. I have a rare genetic disorder that prevents me from gaining weight. I'm blind in one eye and have limited vision in the other. In high school I had two major surgeries, complete with blood transfusions. A simple cold can put me in bed for two weeks.

My condition has yet to be understood by the medical community. It's so rare that only two other people in the world have it. We're not sure what the future holds or how long we'll live.

Right now there's no cure. When I was thirteen, I joined a University of Texas genetic study directed by Dr. Abhimanyu Garg. He believes I have a form of neonatal progeroid syndrome, which causes accelerated aging, fat loss from my face and body, and tissue degeneration. Someday I'd like this medical mystery to be called The Lizzie Syndrome.

There's no hiding my condition—or hiding from it. You only have to look at me to know I'm different, because even though I eat small meals all day, I'm probably the thinnest person you'll ever see.

A lot has been written about me. Some of it's true, and some of it isn't. No, I don't have an eating disorder. My parents do not starve me. Yes, I weigh the same as a second grader. If I gain even one pound I get really excited. I've been called the world's slimmest woman. I can't imagine what being overweight feels like, but I can tell you my weight has been an issue my whole life.

Being stared at and singled out is something I've had to deal with my whole life. People who don't know me have targeted me with hateful, hurtful remarks. Imagine being hated or laughed at because you can't gain weight. But I have an amazing family and great friends who love and support me and are always there for me. They stand up for me when I'm singled out and love me unconditionally.

We are each unique—from the color of our hair to the tone of our voice, we're different from one another. Even identical twins have some differences. The trouble is, our differences are all some people see, which is kind of funny, because I think we're more alike than we're different.

I've spent years wanting to look like everyone else, but it didn't happen. Instead, I had to learn to love and accept myself just as I am. I stopped listening to what other people said and started making a life for *myself*. I've discovered what it means to find my purpose in life, my passion. Each new day is an opportunity I'm grateful for.

My life is exciting. I share my story in person with hundreds of teens and young adults across the country. I do guest appearances on TV: *The Today Show, Inside Edition,* Australia's *Sunday Night,* Germany's *Explosiv,* and now *Dr. Drew.* Sharing my story is my calling, the way I help others.

If I had never looked past the anger and hurt and embraced who I really am, I would have missed these opportunities. As I look back over my struggles, I can see that God was present. I just didn't always understand that.

My faith in God has helped me in every aspect of my life, but I promise not to preach at you or tell you what to believe. That's up to you. I can only tell my story truthfully, and because God has had a huge starring role, I talk about him a lot. Without him, I can't imagine that you would be interested in hearing much about me.

Each day we're given an opportunity to discover our purpose and to prepare to live as best we can. As long as I have faith in God, a smile on my face, and genuine pride in who I am, everything else will happen on schedule. The same is true for you. If you haven't yet discovered your purpose, that's OK—it will come.

During my really dark days, I could never have imagined being as happy as I am today. No, my life isn't perfect. And yes, others' opinions matter. But what matters most is that I'm living my destiny. The secret to my success is that I recognize and embrace my own God-given uniqueness. Life isn't always easy, but this is the only life I've known. I've learned a lot along the way, and I want to share what I've learned.

I hope you stick around.

Reflections

- *Do you spend time thinking about what your life is like now and how you hope it will be?*

- *Do you wish your life was different? How?*

- *Do you have a special dream?*

A Prayer to Share

Dear God,

I'm so excited! Today I get to share my story with some pretty special people, and I have so much to tell them. I know in my heart that you're right here with us. Help us see and appreciate our many blessings!

Thank you,

Lizzie

CHAPTER TWO

Why Me?

*God is faithful, and he will not let you be tested beyond your
strength, but with the testing he will also provide the way out
so that you may be able to endure it.*
1 Corinthians 10:13

My aunt calls me Sunshine because I always have a
smile on my face. Often I'm asked if something wonderful just happened. My answer is yes! Something
wonderful happens every day, even when we're not paying attention.

I love to laugh. One of the things I get from my dad is my
sense of humor. He has the timing of a professional comedian.
Being able to tell a joke and appreciate good humor has taught
me to be quick on my feet and to laugh at myself and my situation. But it isn't always easy to remember to laugh or even smile
when life is hard.

It's common to feel we have to understand everything. We

want to know why bad things happen, what we did to "deserve" them. At one time or another we've each wondered, *Why me? Why do bad things always happen to me? Why must I have another disappointment?*

☼ *It's spring break and all my friends are going on vacation. Well, except me. I have to stay home.*

☼ *I can't believe I have curly hair. I hate it. I want my hair to be long and straight.*

☼ *I can't believe I have straight hair. I hate it. I want my hair to be curly.*

☼ *Why does my brother have autism? It's so not fair to me.*

☼ *Why does my mother have to work?*

☼ *Why doesn't our family have more money?*

☼ *Why does my life have to be so boring?*

Or, in my case, *why can't I look more like the other girls? Why can't I be healthier? If I have to look so different and have this syndrome, then why isn't my immune system stronger? Why is it so easy for me to get sick? Why do I have to be blind in one eye?*

In high school I watched other people seem to effortlessly sail through their days. It just seemed so unfair. No matter how carefully I planned my life, something unexpected would get in the way.

It could be something small and annoying like running out of time to study for a test, hating the way my hair looks, or losing my favorite bracelet—again. Or it could be something huge and scary, something I couldn't control. While others were rushing around having fun, I was stuck in the doctor's office or the emergency department.

I often found myself wondering where God was in all of this. Was he even paying attention? Did he know how hard life was for me? What was the purpose behind this pain and uncertainty? I didn't *want* to give up on God, but sometimes I secretly wondered if he had given up on me.

Everyone seemed happier than I was. They certainly were healthier. Being so sick on top of looking so different was a huge recurring *why me*?

I wondered whether my life would ever make sense. I was filled with sadness and unanswered questions. I resented my fragile health, and I was angry because people judged me without knowing me or giving me a chance.

Everyone has problems, so you've probably felt all of those things on at least one occasion. Think about the things that bother you, things you can and can't control. Now write them down in the space below:

Some *why mes* are significant; others, not so much. Either way, what's on your *why me* list is important. Maybe your father died and you miss him, or maybe your family moved to Florida and you miss your friends in Maryland, or maybe your older brother left home to go to college. These kinds of things are not your fault. They're situations you have no control over. You didn't cause them, and you can't change them.

Other things you do have control of. Maybe you've been experimenting with alcohol or are considering doing drugs. Maybe you've made some bad decisions.

No life is perfect. If you don't believe me, well, ask around: "Hey, is your life perfect?" Guaranteed, if the person feels like venting or sharing, you'll get an earful. Maybe his little brother is driving him crazy. Or she failed her driving test. Or he ran out of time to finish last night's homework because he had to clean the kitchen.

They'll tell you that not only is life not perfect—heck, it isn't even fair. They'll assure you that no one can imagine how many problems they have, and that those problems are nothing to joke about.

"The World's Ugliest Woman" Video

I used to wake up dreading the routine stares and whispers from strangers. Having to deal with all of that on a regular basis was tough in itself, but little did I know, it was about to get a lot worse—and all in the blink of an eye.

One day while I was in high school, I was playing around on YouTube instead of doing my homework. I was looking for some good music, but instead I stumbled on a video of a very familiar

young girl. In what would turn out to be one of the biggest turning points of my life, I clicked on a link to open the eight-second video.

To my utter surprise and horror, the video—which had over 4 million hits, thousands of comments, and no sound—was called "The World's Ugliest Woman."

They were talking about me.

The pain I felt is indescribable. Imagine someone posting your picture on the Internet and labeling you the world's ugliest person. Now add thousands strangers giving you tips on how to hurt yourself because of your appearance. How would that make you feel?

I kept asking myself, *how dare they? How dare they tell me to put a bag over my head so people wouldn't have to see my ugly face? How dare they ask why my parents didn't abort such an ugly monster? How dare they offer tips on how to kill myself?*

There was no way to remove the video. The mere thought of someone having those thoughts sickened me. I thought about punishing them. I wanted them to know how much they had hurt me, to feel the pain I felt. Then I decided that, rather than sink to their level, I'd fight the video with my accomplishments.

Before I did anything else, though, I had to tell my parents. I didn't want to—I wanted to protect them from the video more than I wanted to protect myself from it. I was afraid it would hurt them even more than it hurt me.

And yes, they were very upset, but they automatically went into parent mode and tried to get the video removed. But ironically, as bad as it was, the video brought us closer: We decided as a family to use this situation as motivation to work harder. This was just another bump in the road, and together we would fight through it without retaliating.

What's the Point of Pain?

Why must we go through so many painful experiences?

Actually, I'm not sure. No matter how you look at it, some situations just don't seem fair. Some days life doesn't make sense and you just have to ask for help, change what you can, and pray about the rest. But while you're doing all that, how do you get through it emotionally? Here are some things you can do while you're working your way though any situation:

- ☼ **Don't focus on your pain.** It's OK to feel pain and grieve a loss, but don't focus on the tears. My dad has always told me I'm allowed to have one good cry, and then I have to look for the positive side. My mom has a similar method of helping me move forward. She gives me a few days of feeling sorry for myself and having her help me, and then I need to get out of bed and start making myself feel better.

- ☼ **Be around people.** Sometimes when we're really feeling down, people bring us happiness by making us laugh or just letting us know they care. But they can't do that if you're locked away in your room. Find people to be around, and let them embrace you.

- ☼ **Find something to laugh about.** Did you know that laughing reduces stress hormones and increases and releases endorphins? Endorphins are hormones that reduce pain and cheer us up. It turns out that old saying is true—laughter really is the best medicine. It's important to laugh no matter what kind of day you're having, but it can be really hard to laugh when you're stressed out. So force yourself. You heard me: When you least feel like it, force yourself to laugh for at least fifteen minutes every day. You don't have to wait for something funny to happen. Just smile and go, "Ha, ha, ha." Research has shown that fake laughing sort of tricks the body into releasing the same endorphins it would if you were really laughing, which makes you feel better. No matter what you're going through, resisting the urge to laugh isn't going to make you feel better.

☼ ***No one can (or should) handle everything alone.*** Ask for help. Choose a compassionate and thoughtful person who cares about you, someone whose advice you can respect even if it isn't what you want to hear. I'm lucky to have two wonderful parents, and I hope you do too. I pray you have at least one person you trust, someone who loves you no matter what.

Maybe you're afraid your mom or dad won't welcome what you have to say. I hope you're wrong. I hope they surprise you when the time comes. But if you're right, or if you feel you have no one to turn to, perhaps a teacher or an aunt or a friend's mother or father is ready to welcome you with compassion and love. All you have to do is ask.

☼ ***Cultivate a grateful heart.*** Count your blessings—pretty much every situation could be worse, so be grateful it's not.

Not all problems are created equal, but they're all meaningful. I can't tell you why bad things happen to good people or that the bad things have a purpose. I *can* tell you that some problems can be better understood if we accept responsibility where we should.

Pain forces you to make the time and effort to know yourself and to learn how to deal with problems when what you really want to do is stay in bed. All problems aren't the same, but some things are true about all of them: It's what you do with your struggles that matters. If you're involved in a situation that needs attention, ignoring it won't make it go away. Neither will filling yourself with anger and frustration or blaming others and feeling sorry for yourself. But loving yourself *does* work. Accepting yourself and making a plan *does* work.

I hope you never have to go through what I did, but remember, God never promised life would be easy. He did promise that his grace will transform the meaning and direction of your life. Believing he loves you will change your life as it has changed the lives of others through the centuries. His message is constant, his love unwavering.

Reflections

💜 *Do you think others' lives are better than yours? Why?*

💜 *Think about the last time something went wrong. How did you handle it? Did you accept responsibility where you should? Did you make a plan for next time?*

💜 *Whom do you trust with your secrets?*

A Prayer to Share

Dear God,

Thank you for all you give us. Today could be a great day, but I've been feeling a little down. I'm sort of worrying about everything. I know I take my blessings for granted—I forget just how much I have to be grateful for.
I promise to do better. I know I can trust you and that I have a lot to be thankful for. Thanks for listening.

Love,

Lizzie

CHAPTER THREE

A New Start

The Lord does not see as mortals see; they look on the
outward appearance, but the Lord looks on the heart.
1 Samuel 16:7

For years my goal was to look like everyone else. I had it all figured out: If I looked more normal, other people would like me. If other people liked me, I could like myself.

I couldn't go to school, the grocery store, a restaurant, or a theme park without people stopping dead in their tracks to look me up and down or point at me. You'd think after years and years of this, it would get easier. But it didn't.

I tried to ignore the stares, but it was getting harder and harder. Despite my best efforts, I still saw the same old me when I looked in the mirror. Great hair and a cute smile, but nothing else had changed.

I made the varsity cheerleading squad my sophomore year in high school. I loved cheering and all the fun things it involved, but sometimes I doubted myself because I didn't feel like I was as pretty as the other girls on the team. For a long time I didn't let my personality come out because the other girls intimidated me. I was letting the negative side of my syndrome take over.

No matter how much I prayed, I never woke up looking like everyone else. I tried to disguise myself, but none of the brand-name cool clothes fit my tiny body. I thought if I could have just one day without being stared at or judged because of my looks, everything would magically change. But it didn't happen.

I grew tired of letting strangers define me. I knew inside I was a great girl with a fun personality. I was ready to start defining *myself* as the smart, fun-loving, and courageous girl I knew I was.

I began to wonder if I could like myself just as I was. Could I accept my appearance? Could I stop waiting for other people to love me and, well, just love myself? Could I change the way I thought about life? Could I start today?

The answer—the amazing answer—was *yes*. I *could* stop thinking about what's wrong with me and concentrate on what's right. My appearance is only a tiny piece of who I am, and I needed to stop letting people judge my entire character by it. I couldn't change the way I looked, but I could show others all there is to like about me. I could stop waiting and start living. I could love myself out loud.

I didn't have some big "ah-ha" moment that inspired me to find a way to love and accept myself. I simply ran out of the energy to hate myself. It takes a lot of effort to be upset all the time.

I was ready to show the world how to treat me.

Start at the Top

During my junior year of high school—even before I saw the You-Tube video—I decided to use my energy in a new and different way. First, I started a list of things that make me happy and that I'm grateful for:

Lizzie's LIST

. . . .

☼ *Family who love me no matter what*

☼ *My dogs, Bitsy and Sadie*

☼ *Getting a good grade on a test*

☼ *Spending time with my friends*

☼ *My MP3 player*

☼ *Positive people who want to share their lives with me*

☼ *A God who loves me unconditionally*

What's on your list? Write them here.

Twelve THINGS I'M GRATEFUL FOR

I kept adding things to my list. If I was having a bad day, just reading my list put a smile on my face. I quickly realized that it's impossible to feel sad and thankful at the same time, so being grateful almost immediately changed how I thought and felt about everything.

Yes, nasty hurtful remarks still hurt my feelings, but the hurt didn't last as long because I was beginning to separate others' opinions from my own. The world around me didn't change, but instead of focusing on others' negative opinions or noticing only what made me unhappy, I made it a daily priority to find something to be grateful for. I was no longer playing the waiting game or allowing others to determine how my day went.

Ask God for Help

Next, I started a morning routine of praying before I got out of bed. Connecting with God through prayer seemed natural; after all, I was raised by parents who took me to church every week and made sure I understood that God loves me just like he loves everyone. I thought I had a relationship with him, but all I was really doing was showing him a wish list. That's not having a relationship with God—it's treating him like he's Santa Claus.

For my new morning prayer time, I didn't want to just recite formal prayers (although I love the beautiful formal prayers like the Our Father and the Hail Mary). I didn't want to simply recite my wish list, either. Instead, I started sharing my deepest feelings and desires and thoughts. I told God what was going on and how I was feeling. As I recounted events, if I realized I was blaming others, I'd stop and start over. God's great when it comes to letting us have a do-over.

I prayed that my family and friends would have a good day, and I thanked God for putting them in my life. I asked God to help me focus on what I needed to get done instead of falling into the temptations of social networking or texting my friends to find out the latest gossip. I began to understand myself and others better, to fully appreciate God's faithful love for me, and to express my love for him.

Gratitude is self-fulfilling. It fills our hearts with joy. Whenever I heard myself complaining, I stopped and reconsidered what I wanted to say. These conversations with God were changing my inner thoughts. I was training myself to see the positive things in my life and to thank God for them. Every day it got easier to notice my blessings.

My conversations with God didn't end there. I talked to him throughout the day. Brief moments between classes and walking to and from school were prayer opportunities. I realized that any time can be a special time in God's presence. The more I looked for positive things, the more I noticed, like the sky and the flowers blooming all around me. The more I noticed, the more conscious I was that God is everywhere. I wondered whether everyone notices his glory.

The more we understand God's love for us, the more we will want to spend time with him. The more time we spend in his presence, the greater our joy and the greater our peace.

Smile, Smile, Smile

As I said in Chapter 2, smiles and laughter make you happy. I made a conscious effort to smile more whether I felt like it or not. The more I smiled, the better I felt, and soon it became a habit. I no longer had to *try* to smile all the time—it had become part of me.

The world around me wasn't changing, but I was. People still pointed and stared and made comments, and rude remarks still hurt my feelings. But now I had something to do with these feelings. I had a lot to be grateful for and a lot to smile about, and I had the list to prove it!

We all need to love and value ourselves today, to start living right now instead of waiting until things are perfect. No matter what you've believed about yourself or what others tell you, I have a message for you: *Loving God and being open to him will change your life.* Even the smallest step toward God will be rewarded by his grace.

You can find your own path to happiness by connecting to the presence of God through prayer. Commitment on your part is all it takes. God is willing to meet you where you are right now.

God wants you to know you're loved.

Reflections

💜 *Name four things you wish were different about your life right now.*

💜 *Name one thing you've been putting off. Why are you procrastinating?*

💜 *What's the most important thing you want God to know about you?*

A Prayer to Share

Dear God,

Having you to confide in makes a huge difference in my life. I know you hear the prayers of all who turn to you, of all who come to you in need. Thank you for loving us no matter what we tell you.

Love,

Lizzie

CHAPTER FOUR

Loving Ourselves

So God created humankind in his image,
in the image of God he created them.
Genesis 1:27

Spending time with God each morning was a positive change. On unhappy mornings, I'd simply be still and listen. The quiet time was as helpful and productive as the days I'd ramble on and on about my life, my hopes and dreams, and things that had gone wrong. I began feeling more peaceful and patient and less angry during the day. Things didn't bother me quite as much. I was more relaxed and in a better place.

But I still had work to do: I needed to accept myself and build my self-esteem. Counting my blessings was becoming a habit, and it helped keep me smiling, but sometimes I was still overly concerned with my appearance. One of my biggest mistakes was comparing myself to others. When I would see one of my friends or a girl I didn't know, I'd automatically think, *her hair is way better than mine,* or I'd start comparing our clothes or makeup.

It started clicking in my head that I was the one causing all those bad thoughts. It was all in *my* head—and *I* was the only one who could change that. Every time I compared myself to someone else, I'd stop and tell myself at least one good thing about myself to change the negative to a positive. If I saw a girl who looked better in her jeans than I did, I'd tell myself, *well at least I'm having a really good hair day!* Becoming conscious of all the time I was wasting comparing myself to others really helped change the way I thought of myself.

It was time to change my inner thoughts, time to stop blaming other people for my unhappiness, and time to stop blaming myself. I wanted to be able to turn a switch and *presto!* be self-confident, but of course it didn't happen that way. It was more like watering a plant and waiting for the flowers to bloom.

Early one morning I asked God to help me change how I thought about myself. I was getting better at seeing the positive, but it was still too easy for me to believe the negative.

I imagined this really huge boulder sitting in the road in front of me. The boulder represented my negative thoughts. I was either going to have to climb over that boulder or push it out of my way. I wasn't sure how I was going to do that; what I did know was that I wanted to be on the other side.

I decided to start by taking inventory of all my good qualities. I knew I had them, but I usually only thought about them one at a time. That was fine, but I also needed The Big Picture, so I decided to write them down so I could see them all at once. Here's what I came up with:

Lizzie's LOVE-MYSELF LIST

I have long hair.

I have a nice smile.

I'm interesting.

I have a good sense of style.

I have a great sense of humor.

I love meeting new people.

I'm loyal.

I'm dependable.

I'm fun to be around.

I'm honest.

I'm thoughtful.

I like to share my story.

I'm a great friend.

I'm willing to help those in need.

I'm determined.

I'm ambitious.

Seeing everything I wrote on my list was hard to believe at first. Doubts kept sneaking in, but I kept reminding myself that each item was true and that I had to learn to believe it.

Now it's your turn. What do you love about *your*self? It can be anything! It can be your intelligence, your smile, or how you remember to always say thank you or hold the door for the person behind you. It can be your organizational skills, your excellent memory, your kindness to others, your honesty.

It can be your long eyelashes, how great your hair looks in a ponytail, how high you can jump on your bed, or the sound of your laugh. Anything! Think about your accomplishments. On the next page, make a list of the things you're good at—your talents and your skills. Think of compliments you've received. Don't worry about sounding conceited—we're all entitled to a little conceited time.

If you have trouble getting started, ask someone you're close to for help. Ask what he or she likes about you and go from there. And once you get going, it'll get easier because each idea will spark another.

Your LOVE-MYSELF LIST

When you're happy with your list—for now—read it over and over until it becomes part of you. The more you recognize and believe in what's on your list, the easier it will be to change how you feel about yourself. It's going to take time to build your list and your self-esteem, and your journey may be bumpy. Maybe this will help: *You were created in God's image.* Remind and reassure yourself of that.

Use each item on your list to come up with new ways to use your abilities and talents. You don't have to wait until next semester or until you're older or until you've made some changes—you can love yourself right now.

Whenever you feel overwhelmed or like you're not good enough, thinking about your list of all of your wonderful qualities will get your attention going in a new direction. It will also help you project confidence throughout the day. Hold your head up, smile, and believe in yourself. Be your own best positive example.

Remember, it only takes one person to change your life. Be that person!

Reflections

💜 *Were you surprised by the number of items on your list?*

💜 *Were you surprised by anything you put on your list? If so, why?*

💜 *What will you do the next time you start feeling bad about yourself?*

A Prayer to Share

Dear God,

My heart is filled with gratitude for the great people who are willing to share their lives and happiness with me. Their joy becomes my joy. Thank you for putting them in my life. Thank you for this day!

Love,

Lizzie

CHAPTER FIVE

Change of Mind

The human mind plans the way, but the Lord directs the steps.
Proverbs 16:9

What do you want? Where are you going? Do you want a different life? Why? What are you doing about it? Are you willing to try something else?

To help piece together what real beauty means to you, use each item on your list as a tool to build a more beautiful you. Think about your abilities and talents, and come up with new ways to use them. And guess what? You don't have to wait until next semester. You can love yourself *right now*. You can change how you feel about yourself *while you're writing the list*. And whenever you feel overwhelmed or like you're not good enough, think about the list and all of your wonderful qualities.

Like everything in life, building your list and your self-esteem will take time. It's going to take practice to believe your version of beauty. Maybe this will help: *You were created perfectly in God's image.* Sometimes you have to remind and reassure yourself of that. I know I do.

The journey to building your version of beauty may be bumpy. That's OK. Just keep your eye on your destination, which isn't to be outwardly "pretty"; it's to be kind and caring, to have a purpose, and to be confident in your own skin—and that's beautiful!

How Do You Feel?

Many of my problems were completely out of my control. For example, I felt left out and misunderstood, but just because I knew why I felt that way didn't mean I could do anything about it. If I couldn't fix the reason, did that mean I'd always feel like this? Could I ever be happy?

I decided to sit down with pen and paper and ask myself a bunch of questions about my life. Then I answered each question as honestly as I could.

After I finished, I stared at my answers and realized that the only way to turn my life around was to make changes. I couldn't do anything about the old memories and hurts, but I could look beyond them to the good things. And when I started paying attention to the positives, the bad things seemed to fade a little more each day.

Now it's your turn. Turn off your phone, TV, and computer, and find a quiet place to write. Ask yourself the following questions, and think about each one before you answer it. There are no right or wrong answers in general, but there are right and wrong answers for you. But don't worry—if you're honest, you'll answer correctly.

Do you often feel left out? Why or why not?

Do you ever feel misunderstood? If so, what makes you feel that way?

Think about an argument you had with your mom, your sibling, or your best friend. What could you have done differently?

Are you ever afraid you'll never be happy? Why or why not?

Do old memories and hurts continue to haunt you? Name one. Why does this still bother you? What would it take to make it truly part of your past?

Do you have someone to discuss these thoughts with, someone you trust? If yes, name that person.

Are you failing in school? If yes, why?

What can you do to turn your life around today?

What do you spend most of your time doing? Do you ever find yourself procrastinating instead of doing?

Do you believe each person has a purpose?

What's your passion?

What do you want to be different in your life right now? Next week? Next year?

What's your idea of the perfect day?

How do you feel about God?

Do you pray? Why or why not?

Do you go to church? Why or why not?

Name three people you blame for your troubles.

Do you ever blame yourself for your troubles?

Many of these questions are the kind we don't want to deal with, and answering them can be difficult. But the answers matter.

Reflections

♥ *Did answering the questions in this chapter make you see anything in a different way?*

♥ *Did any of your answers make you see that you actually can control something you thought you couldn't?*

♥ *Did any of your answers make you see that something you thought you could control is really strictly in God's hands?*

A Prayer to Share

Dear God,

Please be with me. Sometimes I'm frightened by change. Today I need to know I'm not alone and that you know what is in my heart. Thank you for this new beginning and for answering my prayers. Please help me to recognize and accept new opportunities, to learn, and to grow.

Love,

Lizzie

CHAPTER SIX

Forgiving Trespasses

Be kind to one another, tender-hearted,
forgiving one another,
as God in Christ has forgiven you.
Ephesians 4:32

I dedicated a lot of days to asking *why me.* I even got angry at God for allowing me to be different. I couldn't comprehend why he'd want me to go through struggle after struggle for no apparent reason. I knew in my heart that I had an amazing family, supportive friends, and a strong will to keep going, but it felt like I was continually being knocked down.

In public, people treated me as if I was some kind of foreign creature. Makeup and new clothes didn't change that. And now, to top it all off, strangers were attacking me on the Internet. No matter where I went, I couldn't escape the criticism.

My resentment was building. I was so frustrated at everyone for judging me. I wanted to scream from the top of a mountain,

"I'm normal just like you!!" I had a tight grip on every memory of everyone who had made me feel bad about myself. Every stare, every hurtful comment, and every mean e-mail was like a paper cut—quick and sometimes hard to see, but it hurts until it's healed.

Even God was on my angry list. No matter how much I prayed, he wasn't making my life easier. I wanted a quick fix—I wanted God to make my syndrome disappear. It never occurred to me that even if you don't have a syndrome and you look like everyone else, you still struggle.

Then one evening our family decided to go to the movies. We stopped to get a couple of buckets of popcorn. (We're a popcorn-loving family.) Everything was great until a group of people started staring and pointing at me. I wanted to pretend they weren't there. But as I was turning away, my dad walked right up to them.

Instead of scolding them for making fun of his daughter, he simply said he was going to pray for them. Then he walked away. Later, he told me that people who do things in a mean spirit need our prayers the most. They need a positive light to remind them that their actions can hurt other people. I'll never forget how impressed I was by my father's actions. He taught me a lot that day.

And that's when all the puzzle pieces started fitting together: I wouldn't be able to move on with my life or be happy with myself until I forgave everyone who had hurt me.

First, I needed to get things right with God. I stopped seeing my syndrome as a big, garish flashing sign that said *curse* and started seeing it as a beautiful, brightly colored sign that said *blessing*. God showed me through my dad that all the people who had judged me and made me feel bad about myself were, in fact, the ones who needed prayer the most.

It was time I learned to forgive those who had trespassed against me.

Forgiving Others

To forgive is to *choose* to let go of resentment, anger, and thoughts of revenge and get on with your life. After that night at the movies, I began praying for and forgiving all the people who had made comments about me on YouTube. Anyone who stared at me and anyone who trespassed against me was on my prayer list. I let go of the past and forgave the people who had singled me out.

I'd pray for them every night, asking God to help me truly forgive them and asking him to be a positive light in their lives. Just like they don't know my story, I don't know theirs—so I can't judge their character by just one action.

At one of my elementary school speeches, a third-grader asked whether I'd forgiven the people who posted the video. I was surprised and taken aback at his very well-thought-out question. No one had ever asked me that.

Do I forgive them? I felt very proud when I realized I could tell him with complete confidence that yes, I do. If I don't forgive them, I'll always feel caught up in the past and have a feeling of dread and dislike for each of those people. There's no reason to hold on to so much animosity. By embracing forgiveness, I found a sense of peace that was missing.

I'll never forget the YouTube video. It will always be part of my life. But by letting go of my feelings of anger and revenge, I've taken away its power. I don't know why those people did what they did or why so many other people felt compelled to add their own hurtful comments but, following my dad's example, I pray for them.

Don't get me wrong—I'm not saying the video doesn't matter. But you can forgive someone who has hurt you without excusing the act.

The pain and hurt we absorb as a result of another person's action can help us become more understanding and kinder. Because of what those people did to me, I would never do something like that to anyone else.

We all need to learn to forgive. If you're having a hard time with this—if you're thinking that whoever did you wrong is unforgivable—think again. God forgives every one of our sins every single day. If God can forgive us, we can find it in our hearts to forgive the people who trespass against us.

Part of my mission in life is to help others let go of hate and hostility, to move past the resentment and negative feelings and understand how not forgiving impacts the quality of our lives. I can be Lizzie the Ugliest Girl, or I can be Lizzie the author of *Be Beautiful, Be You.*

I choose the latter.

Asking Others to Forgive You

What if *you're* the one who needs forgiveness?

Look at the situation honestly, asking yourself what happened and whom you hurt. Don't judge yourself. We all make mistakes, even when we don't mean to.

Have you said or done something to hurt or wound someone? Are you sorry? Do you want to make amends? Do you want to ask them for forgiveness? What do you hope to accomplish? Have you prayed about the situation? Are you ready to admit what happened? Do you regret your words or actions?

Consider what you'll say. Don't make excuses—simply say you're sorry, that you wish it hadn't happened, and that if you could take it back you would.

You can't force others to listen to you or forgive you. That's up to them. Each of us has the right to decide whether to forgive. Give them the time and space to do so, and don't get mad if they refuse.

Whatever the outcome, forgiveness is a gift you give yourself.

Reflections

- 💜 *Do you feel guilty about something? What is it? What can you do to make the guilt go away?*

- 💜 *Think about someone who hurt you. Can you forgive that person?*

- 💜 *Think about someone you've hurt. Have you let that person know you're truly sorry and asked them to forgive you?*

A Prayer to Share

Dear God,

I need help forgiving those who hurt me. I'm angry, and it makes me sad to be singled out. Sometimes I just want them to suffer so they'll know what if feels like. I know this is wrong and that I need to let go of the resentment in my heart and forgive them even if they don't ask forgiveness. Help me forgive others as you forgive me. Fill me with your understanding.

Love,

Lizzie

CHAPTER SEVEN

Find Your Passion

Do not be conformed to this world, but be transformed by the renewing of your minds, so that you may discern what is the will of God—what is good and acceptable and perfect.
Romans 12:2

One of the most memorable steps on my journey to self-discovery was accepting an invitation to share my story with a group of high school freshmen. At first I refused, but the offer was extended again. Everyone around me was encouraging me to share my unique story and my successes.

I have to be honest—the last thing I wanted to do was stand on a stage and have an entire audience focus their attention on me. All my old fears immediately presented themselves. But after a lot of encouragement—and even more prayer—I finally accepted the invitation.

That night I sat down at my computer and asked myself, if I were in the audience, what would I want to hear? The idea I most wanted to get across was not how to simply live with problems; I wanted to say, yes, we all have problems, but when life knocks us down we need to get up—again and again if necessary—and live the way we were meant to live.

I decided the best way to get my point across would be to talk about my life and how I got where I am today. The audience would know just by looking at me that I'm different, so I'd start by explaining my condition—how my body is unable to store fat and maintain muscle, so I need to eat all day, every day.

Because God is a huge part of my life, I'd also talk about my faith. Finally, I'd put them at ease by focusing on what we have in common. I'd say that I care about my friends and worry about grades just like they do. Then, hoping to make them laugh, I'd tell them I love to shop.

Once I knew what I wanted to say, the words flowed naturally, and soon my speech was finished. I felt great, because now I was sure I had something important to say. But on the day of the speech, I was beyond nervous. I couldn't believe I'd let myself be talked into doing this. I worried about my appearance and my voice—would I even be able to speak? Would they listen, or would they leave? I was doing better. Did I really need another bad experience?

But before I could leave, I heard my name followed by welcoming applause. As I stood before the audience of 400 students, I forgot to look down at my carefully prepared speech. Instead, I told them how it feels to be the outsider everywhere I go. I talked to them from my heart. And they responded well. Sometimes they were quiet, hanging on to every word. Other times I saw heads nodding in understanding. There were even a few laughs and a bunch of chuckles.

At the end, they applauded loudly and, to my amazement, stood. My first talk had been a giant success.

At that moment two things happened: My heart filled with an overwhelming sense of pride, and I recognized my calling: I wanted to become a motivational speaker.

And to think I almost said no to the opportunity!

How to Find Your Passion

Getting in touch with your life's purpose isn't all that hard. Discovering your calling is all about paying attention to what's important to you, how you want to spend your days, and how you see yourself. You have to be willing to put some serious time into finding the answer and then questioning the answer by asking yourself whether it feels right. You can be called to do more than one thing, so don't limit your thinking to only one idea.

Passion and purpose go hand in hand. What do you like to do? I mean *really* like to do? What will fill your days with so much interest and excitement that you forget what time it is? What can you picture yourself doing every day without losing interest?

Think about your answers to those questions. Ask yourself whether this passion is something you're good at or seem to have a gift for. It's great to want to be a singer, but if you can't sing a note without people clapping their hands over their ears in protest, chances are you should keep looking.

If you weren't able to answer the questions, that doesn't mean you don't have a passion. It just means you haven't found it yet, and that's OK. As long as you remain open to new experiences, you'll find it—and when you find it, you'll know it.

Write a Mission Statement

Once you've identified your passion and purpose, spend some alone time writing a mission statement. A mission statement answers the question, *Why was I created?* One of the first steps in starting an organization or business is to write a mission statement. But mission statements aren't just for businesses and organizations—they're also for people who want to be sure they fulfill their purpose on Earth.

I continually meet teens who have no idea how fortunate they are. They're talented and fun to be around. They can be good listeners or leaders, and they're full of energy and enthusiasm. Trouble is, they don't recognize these great qualities in themselves.

My job, as I see it, is to help them recognize their gifts. I truthfully praise them and point out that because they have been given this unique set of gifts, they have a responsibility to use them wisely. They have a responsibility to show up for themselves, because one day they will hold themselves accountable for their own successes or failures.

How did I get all of that into a one-sentence mission statement? It took some work, but here it is:

> *I want to help people recognize that they have a unique set*
> *of gifts and a responsibility to use those gifts wisely.*

When I'm successful, I love watching their faces light up. They get it, and I couldn't be happier, because when I motivate them, *they* motivate *me*.

Some days I remember to share these same messages with myself. When I work hard and do a good job, I try to acknowledge my efforts. When I achieve a goal, I spend some time enjoying the feeling of accomplishment. I treat myself the same way I treat other people and the way I'd like them to treat me.

Now it's your turn. Here are some questions to get you started:

💜 *Whom do you want to help?*

💜 *Are you creative?*

💜 *A problem solver?*

💜 *Quiet?*

💜 *Outgoing?*

💜 *Spiritual?*

💜 *A learner?*

💜 *A doer?*

💜 *Is there anything else about you—a special talent, a personality trait, anything—you should incorporate into your mission statement?*

Use your answers to write a one-sentence mission statement here:

Live Your Beliefs, Live Your Life

Chances are, God hasn't chosen an ordinary or boring life for you. If your life is the "same old, same old," maybe it's time to rethink your relationship with your Creator. Start with a good prayer conversation. And don't forget, conversation isn't just talking—it's also listening.

There's a whole lot of world out there to be discovered, and your job is to find your place in it. Remember, just one success will give you something to build on.

Sometimes it's just about getting started and seeing where the action takes you.

Reflections

💜 *Can you go an entire day without saying "can't"?*

💜 *Finish this sentence: I really want to….*

💜 *Why are some people successful when others aren't?*

A Prayer to Share

Dear God,

I know how patient you've been with me. Time after time you've given me opportunities to recognize my talents. I never knew that one day I'd stand in front of crowds and share my story. Now I understand my life better. I trust you and can't wait to see where you lead me next!

Love,

Lizzie

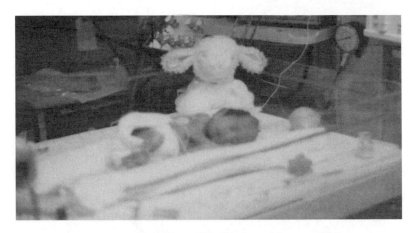

Here I am, only a few days old.

I had to be fed through a tube.

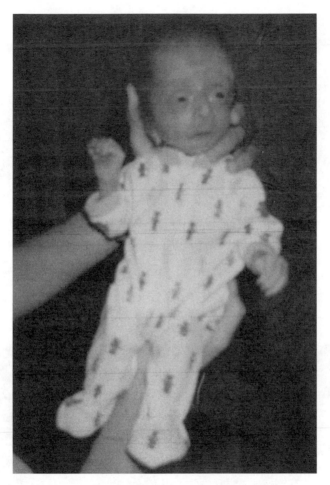

My baby clothes were actually doll clothes.

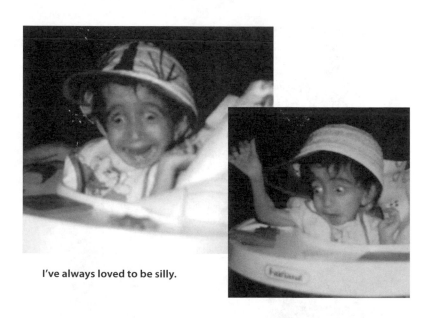

I've always loved to be silly.

My first birthday.

Preparing for an interview on Australia's *Sunday Night*.

Doing a radio interview on *The Bobby Bones Show*.

With Mom and Dr. Drew.

Aunt Stephanie.

Christmas Eve with my family.

My twenty-third birthday with Roman, one of my best friends.

Talking about bullying at an elementary school.

Filming for the National Geographic Channel.

My friend Vickie.

My friends Kia and Jessica.

Bowling with my cousins Andrea, Rebecca, and Cheyanne.

Aunts Lisa and Elia.

Rebecca and Andrea.

My dad.

My brother, Chris.

With Mom at a college baseball game.

My sister, Marina, and my brother, Chris.

National Geographic films dinner with family and friends.

Chris and Marina.

CHAPTER EIGHT

Ready, Set, Goal!

Prepare your work outside,
get everything ready for you in the field;
and after that build your house.
Proverbs 24:27

y parents instilled in me an inner strength that I continue to build on. They taught me by example to never give up, to find solutions to problems, to keep going even when the road seems bumpy, and to take responsibility for myself by setting goals and following through until I achieve them.

I wrote my mission statement and made my first real set of long-term goals when I was in high school. Here they are (and yes, I wrote them down):

☼ *Become a motivational speaker*

☼ *Write a book about my life*

✵ *Graduate from college*

✵ *Have my own family*

By age twenty-one I was in my fifth year of motivational speaking, and my first book had been published in both English and Spanish. I'm now twenty-three, and in a few months I'll walk across a stage to get my college diploma. Oh—and you're reading my second book!

I soon realized, however, that these goals weren't enough. Meeting three of them was a huge accomplishment, but all I could think about was, "What's next?"

It seems to me that too many people haven't spent enough time thinking about what they want to accomplish, and they haven't made a list of goals. That's sort of like planning a trip without any idea of the destination.

If you've already written your mission statement, you know where you want to go. Now you can focus on how to get there. The "how to get there" is a list of goals. Writing them down makes them real, so your list can turn a want into a reality. Start by asking these questions:

1. *What three things do you want to accomplish this week?*

2. *What three things do you want to accomplish by the end of the year?*

3. *What three things do you want to accomplish by your next milestone birthday? (A milestone is a special event in your life, a turning point, like your thirteenth, sixteenth, or eighteenth birthday.)*

Using those lists, take a couple of minutes to think about your top three goals for the next year and your top three goals for further down the road.

Top 3 Goals for the Next Year

Top 3 Goals for Further Down the Road

Now you know what you want to do. All that's left is to figure out how and when to do it.

Sometimes looking at a list of goals can be intimidating or overwhelming—that's natural, and it's OK to feel that way as long as you don't let it stop you.

But how do you actually meet your goal? Map out a detailed plan. First, get some paper and a pen. Any paper or pen will do, but it's also fun to get a cool-looking notebook or journal and a special pen that you use only for this purpose.

For each of your goals, do this:

1. *Write down your goal.*

2. *Get the facts about the big steps it will take to achieve that goal. Do you need to take classes, do some reading on your own, join a group, buy some supplies or equipment? Write down the big steps.*

3. *Now you need to break the big steps into little steps. For example, if you need to take classes to meet your goal, you'll need to find out where they're offered, when they're offered, and how much they cost. If you need to do some reading, you'll need to go to the library. Write down the little steps.*

4. *If you need to break the little steps down into even littler steps, keep breaking them down until you have a complete list of exactly what you need to do.*

5. *Give yourself a timeline. If you tend to procrastinate, give yourself a date by which you want to accomplish each step. Write it in parentheses at the end of the goal. If you're not a procrastinator, choose a date by which you want to reach the halfway point of your goal, and then pick another date to finish. Knowing you have a deadline will give you extra encouragement to get things done.*

Here's an example. If one of your goals is to become more involved at church, this could be your list:

1. *Go to the parish website and read the descriptions of the volunteer opportunities. (May 1)*

2. *Decide which one you'd like to try. (May 3)*

3. *Contact the group leader and ask what you need to do next. (May 10)*

4. *Follow the group leader's instructions. (May 15)*

That's not so hard, is it? You'll get so involved in breaking down your goal into steps, you won't be nervous or intimidated anymore by the time you finish. You'll be so eager to get started, you'll probably want to do step 1 right away!

After I made my list, I started sharing daily goals with my roommate. Every morning we wrote down the things we wanted to get done that day. We kept a tally system, and if we completed all our goals that day, we got one tally. The first to get five points won a reward, which usually had something to do with food because we both love tacos.

If you have a competitive nature like mine, trying to win a tally competition with a friend will help you be more productive even when you don't feel like it.

Reimagine Your Life

Take some time to sit and imagine that you've completed every goal on your list, both short- and long-term. Imagine the obstacles you had to overcome, all the times you wanted to give up but didn't, and all the times you were discouraged but kept pushing forward.

Now think about how you'd feel checking off each goal on your list. Imagine your joy and pride at setting your mind to something and working hard to accomplish it.

Can you see the smile on your face? Think how excited you'd be to share your accomplishments with the people you love. Doesn't just *thinking* about it put a little extra energy in your step?

Now it's time to get to work! Any time you're feeling down or don't think you are going to reach your goal, remind yourself how great it's going to be once you get there.

Reflections

💜 *Do you have one bad habit you wish you could change?*

💜 *What steps would you have to take to change it?*

💜 *Are you willing to map out a plan that will help you take those steps?*

💜 *Are you willing to follow the plan?*

A Prayer to Share

Dear God,

Thank you for giving me the confidence to overcome obstacles. Let me succeed. Teach me to believe in myself and focus on the right thing to do. Help me gather my thoughts and go in the right direction. Yours is the only real path to lasting success. Show me the way.

Love,

Lizzie

CHAPTER NINE

Deal With Disappointment

*Do not worry about anything, but in everything by prayer
and supplication with thanksgiving let your requests
be made known to God. And the peace of God,
which surpasses all understanding,
will guard your hearts and your minds in Christ Jesus.*
Philippians 4:6–7

Living through my unique set of challenges prepared me to help others have a happier, healthier life. Dealing with my own challenges makes it easier to spot the pain and loneliness in other people's eyes. Learning to cope with bullies gives me the courage to stand up for those who are targets. Getting honest with myself helps me understand that not everything I want is good for me or even possible. Sometimes the answer is *no*.

I love what I do, but if I woke up tomorrow and it was all gone I'd be OK. I trust God and believe he alone knows best. If I never stand on another stage in front of a welcoming crowd or do another TV show, I'll know it's because God has chosen another path for me.

Put Things in Perspective

So you haven't gotten everything you want. You asked, but you haven't received. Maybe you worked really hard to pray and set goals, and it just isn't happening.

You may think *no* is the worst thing in the world, but it isn't. Things could be worse. If you stop focusing on your own disappointment and look around, you'll see that there are far worse situations.

We've all wanted something we couldn't get, so I know you understand. Letting yourself become frustrated and angry doesn't work. Neither does dwelling on the failure. We can pout and complain and even whine about the outcome, or we can think about all the opportunities that have come our way and all the success we've had.

I feel your pain, I really do, but not getting everything you want—sometimes the thing you want most—is part of being human. Turns out I'm not going to look like every other girl in my school. Oh, well. God had a different plan.

It's a lot easier to accept the "different plan" when you have high self-esteem—when you love and accept yourself exactly as you are. People with high self-esteem share most or all of the following seven qualities. For each, think about the quality, and then answer the questions.

✩ **_They like themselves._** _Do you like yourself? Why? If you don't like yourself, why not? Make a list of things you can do to fix those things._

✩ **_They honestly assess their personal strengths and weaknesses._** _Do you spend time thinking about your strengths and weaknesses? List three of each. Have they changed over the years? List one way you can strengthen each weakness in the next year._

☼ ***They take responsibility for their choices and actions.*** *Do you usually make good decisions? If you make a mistake, do you blame others, or do you accept responsibility and promise yourself you'll do better next time? Give examples.*

☼ ***They're leaders in their school and community.*** *Do you look for opportunities to take on responsibility? Do you volunteer? If yes, give examples. If no, list three things you're going to do in the next three months to take on responsibility and help others.*

✿ **They put the needs of others first when necessary.** *If a friend or family member needs your help, do you make an effort to be there even if it's inconvenient or you'd rather do something else? If yes, give examples. If no, think of a time in the last year when someone asked for your help. What were your real reasons for saying no? What should you have done? Why?*

✿ **They stand firm in their beliefs.** *Do you avoid situations and behaviors you feel are wrong or will lead to trouble? Do you stand up for what you believe in even when others make it hard? If yes, give examples. If no, write down a situation you're currently in or one that's likely to happen in the next three months. Next, write a plan so you'll be ready to handle it in a way that won't compromise your beliefs.*

☼ ***They're kind and compassionate to themselves as well as others.*** *Are you nice to yourself? Do you give yourself a pat on the back when you do the right thing? Do you forgive yourself when you make a mistake? If yes, give examples. If no, write down three things you can do for yourself this week, and then do them.*

Compare your answers to your Love-Myself List. Do you have the qualities of a person with high self-esteem? If not, you're not reading your Love-Myself list often enough.

As for me, I can answer yes to each item on the list: I like myself. I work hard to honestly evaluate my strengths and weaknesses. I pay attention to what changes I need to make, and I accept responsibility for my choices and my actions. When I'm faced with a problem, I do my best to solve it in a way that doesn't compromise my beliefs. If I make a mistake, I try to own up to it. I do better some days than others. I'm not perfect, not even close.

Having high self-esteem doesn't guarantee that your life will be easy, endlessly happy, and without problems. But it does guarantee that you will be surrounded with love and supported by people who care.

And that changes everything.

Reflections

💜 *What has been your biggest disappointment?*

💜 *How did you deal with it?*

💜 *How will you deal with your next big disappointment?*

A Prayer to Share

Dear God,

I work very hard to get what I want, and I'm very proud of myself. Most of the time that's a good thing, but it can also make disappointment even harder to take if I feel like I'm not getting what I deserve. Please help me see that when I don't get what I want, it will be OK, because you'll be there pointing me in another direction—the right direction.

Love,

Lizzie

CHAPTER TEN

Friends for Life

For if they fall, one will lift up the other;
but woe to one who is alone and falls
and does not have another to help.
Ecclesiastes 4:10

I love my friends. They're a huge part of my life. Finding and keeping good friends takes work, and I put just as much work into *being* a good friend.

Real friends tell you the truth because they have your best interests at heart. My friends and I never sugarcoat or beat around the bush, even if what we have to say is upsetting. Maybe that sounds rude, but it doesn't have to be. You can tell someone the truth without being rude or vindictive. Real friends can tell you upsetting truths in a loving and caring way.

That's what my friends and I do for each other. I value that quality in each of them, and I want to be to be the same kind of friend to them.

My friends and I are loyal, trustworthy, and fun to be around. We hang out, take in a movie, talk on the phone, study, share disappointment, and talk about our heartaches. We celebrate holidays and birthdays and special times, and we support each other during bad times.

Are You a Good Friend?

Friends come in many varieties. There are friends you go to the movies with, and friends you shop with. There are study friends and workout friends, friends who live next door and—if you're lucky—friends who share their innermost thoughts with you.

To have good friends, you have to be a good friend. Take this little quiz to see if you are:

☼ *Do you genuinely care about your friends? How do you show them?*

☼ *Do you make an effort to stay in touch? Give an example.*

☼ *Are you loyal? Give an example.*

☼ *Do you trust your friends? Give an example.*

☼ *Do you tell your friends the truth? Give an example.*

☼ *Do you enjoy being with them? What's your favorite thing to do with your friends?*

Are Your Friends Good Friends?

It can be pretty hard to be happy and in good spirits when you're surrounded by grumpy, complaining people who notice only the negatives in life. It's important to surround yourself with friends who are upbeat and respectful. Answer these questions to see If you have good friends.

☼ *Do your friends make an effort to stay in touch? Give an example.*

✿ Can you be honest with your friends, or do you hold back because you're afraid they'll judge you? Give an example.

✿ Has anyone ever told you that one of your friends isn't being a good friend to you? If yes, how did you handle that? Did you talk it over with someone else?

✿ Have you ever caught a friend in a lie? If yes, how did you handle it?

✿ Are your friends fun to be around, or do they only come around when they want something?

Friendships need attention to survive. Let your friends know how important they are to you. Share your problems, but don't spend hours complaining or whining. Don't talk about yourself constantly—be sure you're asking about their lives.

Good friends are worth the effort it takes to keep them around. Most of the time that's easy to do, but sometimes you'll have disagreements. You might even say you don't have a true friendship until you've had a fight and made up.

When you do have a disagreement, don't ignore the situation. Don't let it fester. Giving each other the silent treatment or refusing to offer or accept an apology will only make the situation worse. Talk things out even if you don't want to. Each of you should have the opportunity to explain your feelings.

Then you need to say, OK, now I know how *you* feel about it, and you know how *I* feel about it. Where do we go from here? How do we fix this? For your friendship to survive, you have to be able to truly move on—that means no grudges.

Fights and struggles make true friendship stronger, so be willing to put up with the rough patches—they're normal. And remember, it's not the differences that matter, but how you resolve them.

Keeping good friends is just as important as finding them. Put forth the effort to maintain well-balanced friendships. Be willing to meet each other halfway.

New Friends

Making new friends isn't difficult. Who are the people you're always happy to see and enjoy being around? Who are the people who think you're fun to be around? Find more people like them.

Remember, you're looking for true friends—don't be friends with anyone just because you think doing so will increase your social ranking at school or work. Find friends whom you simply want to share your life with and who simply want to share their lives with you.

Look for friends at your school, church, community—everywhere. Be willing to introduce yourself to the new girl or guy at church.

Find people who share your interests and like to do the same things you like to do. Common ground is always a good conversation starter. If you're invited out, say yes, and show up with a smile.

In the next month, get to know at least one person you don't know well or who you've noticed doesn't have a lot of friends. If you want other people to give you a chance, you have to give them a chance as well.

People come into our lives for many reasons. Some are positive role models who have much to teach us. The four girls I shared high school with will be forever special to me. We ate lunch together every day at the same table. We grew up at that table. We laughed, got to know each other's families, shared the latest school news, and learned how to be friends.

We hit some milestones together: surviving our teen years, being part of one another's *quinceañeras* (the Hispanic fifteenth-birthday celebration). Our biggest concerns were who was going

to stand with whom at a *quince* or what movie we wanted to see that weekend. My friendship with Rebecca, Abigail, Karina, and Patsy has truly been a blessing.

When It's Time To Say Goodbye

Not all friendships are forever, and that's OK—not all should be. Maybe you've grown apart, or the dynamics have changed. Maybe you no longer share interests, or you have new demands on your time. Sometimes the relationship has become unhealthy, but you've been friends for a long time and you feel obligated to continue the friendship.

We're taught to be forgiving, and it might seem like ending a friendship isn't a very forgiving thing to do. But you can do both at the same time.

If a friendship is no longer working for you, take these steps:

✿ *Decide whether you want to discuss the situation or just end the friendship. Think this over carefully, because restarting friendships can be tricky.*

✿ *Before you make a complete break, think about whether you want to talk occasionally on the phone or exchange holiday and birthday cards.*

✿ *If you decide to end the friendship, be polite but firm when you talk to your friend.*

✿ *Move on.*

Reflections

- *Who are truly your best friends?*

- *Are you best friends to them as well?*

- *Are you in a friendship that isn't healthy anymore and needs to end? What will you do about it?*

A Prayer to Share

Dear God,

I'm so grateful to you for giving me so many wonderful friends. Please watch over each of them and bless them. Thank you, God, for all of my friends.

Love,

Lizzie

CHAPTER ELEVEN

Take Care of Yourself

Beloved, I pray that all may go well with you
and that you may be in good health,
just as it is well with your soul.
3 John 2

usic has always been one of my great loves. One of my favorite things to do on a rainy or cold winter day or is snuggle up and listen to some good music. Put me in a room with dim lighting, a cup of coffee, and my MP3 player—I guarantee that will fix any bad mood or elevate a good one.

I've created mood playlists on my MP3 player so I always have the right kind of music at my fingertips. My homework playlist helps me be more productive. If I'm having a down day or I'm upset about something, I turn on my gospel-music playlist. It never fails to lift my spirits and remind me how blessed I am.

The idea for creating different playlists for different moods came to me before a scheduled surgery. I was nervous and anxious, so I added some upbeat music to my trusty gospel-music list. Listening to my new playlist in the hospital kept me in good spirits and distracted me from the pain. I named the soothing playlist Worship Music.

Everyone should have a set of mood playlists. Look at each song in your collection and think about how listening to it affects your mood. Ask yourself, what does this piece make me feel like? Studying? Getting ready to go to sleep? Just having fun?

Then, put them together. Start with three: one for when you're having a bad day or are stressed out, one for when you're doing your homework, and one for when you're feeling happy and upbeat. Add more as you think of them until you have one for every mood. Be sure to name them so you can find them easily. In addition to Worship Music I have Finals Tunes, Cold Nights, and Book Songs.

Putting together playlists is fun, something you do just for yourself. No matter my mood, it helps to listen to good music. The tunes on my Worship Music playlist inspire me to feel better and remind me that God loves me. That's great medicine for any soul.

Listening to Myself

Some days going into my room, shutting the door, turning on my MP3 player, and connecting with my feelings seems selfish, like something I shouldn't be doing. Before I learned the importance of being true to myself, I struggled with feelings of guilt: *I could be doing something more productive. There's so much need in the world, things I need to do, and instead of doing them I'm sitting here listening to music.*

I changed this view when I realized I can't give to others unless I first give to myself. I can't have compassion for others until I'm compassionate with myself. For example, I was agreeing to too many appearances even though I was trying to maintain my grade average. It was too much to handle. I realized that if I didn't start taking "me time," I'd burn out. I needed regular time to regroup and restore my own levels of energy, and music became important for that time.

Today I pay attention to my own needs and well-being. I make sure I get plenty of rest and have time for things that make me happy. After a particularly busy season, I need a minivacation—time to just hang out and regain my balance, time to pray and reconnect with God and his will.

What Do You Need?

Think about ways you can be more compassionate with yourself. For me, listening to music is huge, but so is reading a good book and walking around the mall.

How do you show compassion to *your*self? Write down at least five simple things—like listening to music—that make you happy:

Read this list often as a reminder to take care of yourself. And then do it!

Reflections

💜 *What is your favorite meaningful song? Why?*

💜 *What is your favorite fun song?*

💜 *If you were allowed to listen to music only for one purpose (like to cheer you up, help you exercise, put you to sleep, or some other purpose), what purpose would you choose? Why?*

A Prayer to Share

Dear God,

I love the way music lifts my spirits, bringing calm and peace into my day. I'm so grateful for those who share their creative talents with us. Thank you for this wonderful gift.

Love,

Lizzie

CHAPTER TWELVE

Feed Your Faith

The sabbath was made for humankind,
and not humankind for the sabbath.
Mark 2:27

J've been going to Mass my entire life, and I consider the Catholic Church to be my second home. My life is immeasurably enriched by my parish. It's a community full of people who love one another and Jesus. I enjoy praying with them and knowing what's going on in their lives. Whenever I'm sick, my mother asks them to pray on my behalf, and knowing so many people are praying for me brings me much comfort.

My parish church is flawlessly beautiful, and just walking inside gives me a feeling of peace. As I kneel and pray, the hushed atmosphere begins to heal my soul and smooth the ragged edges of my week. As I listen to the readings and the homily, I often learn something or am reminded of a truth I'd forgotten. The faint scent of incense reminds me of my history with this community. I celebrated my first Communion, confirmation, and first penance here. I've attended baptisms, weddings, and funerals here. These experiences are an important part of who I am.

But there's a more important reason I go to Mass every week. When I close my eyes, I'm thinking not of the people or the pews, but of the gift I'm about to receive: the source of all that is holy, the meaning of the Mass. Catholics believe that as we gather to pray and sing and listen to Scripture readings, Christ is calling us to his table to receive holy Communion.

Receiving the consecrated Bread and Wine brings healing and peace. We celebrate Jesus' love for us—his life, his death, his resurrection, and our personal relationship with him.

Fall in Love With the Mass

The Church teaches that attending Mass every week will help us feel God's presence, but when we do something automatically every week, we can start to take it for granted. We may even start thinking of it as just another task to check off our to-do list: *clean my bedroom, wash Mom's car, go to church, babysit*. We may even convince ourselves it's OK to skip Mass occasionally—we went last week, and we'll go again next week, so it's OK to do something else this week.

Whether you go to Mass on Sunday or Saturday evening, it should be the highlight of your week. I love to go to Mass on Sundays, but you should go when you'll be able to get the most out of it. Just remember: You shouldn't be working Mass into your busy schedule—you should be planning your busy schedule around Mass.

And you probably already know this, but I'm going to say it anyway: Showing up is only the first step to participating in the Mass. To really live the Mass in a way that brings you closer to God and your community, you have to put your heart and soul into it:

- ☼ *Learn The Order of Mass.* *The parts of the Mass are equally important, and you should understand what's happening in each of them.*

- ☼ *Get to know the prayers and hymns of the Mass.* *Most of us know these prayers and hymns so well we can recite and sing them perfectly while thinking of something altogether different. Don't fall into that trap. Instead, try this: Really think about what the words mean, and each time you pray or sing, do it as if it were your first time.*

- ☼ *Listen carefully to the Scripture readings and the homily.* *The homily helps you apply the day's Scripture readings to your everyday life, but you won't learn anything if you're not paying attention.*

- ☼ *Focus on the Body and Blood of Christ.* *After Communion, it's easy to let your mind wander to all the things you still have to do before Monday. But that's not what this time is for. Kneel or sit silently in prayer, concentrating on the miracle you just received. Reflect on your participation in the eucharistic meal and how it brings you closer to Jesus and the Christian community.*

☼ **Go in peace.** Don't leave the Mass behind when you leave the building—keep it in your heart all week. Your parish bulletin will be a big help with this part. Read the whole thing to learn about volunteer opportunities and parish events that will bring you closer to your community. Remember the prayer requests, and if the bulletin contains a reflection on the readings—sort of a bonus homily—read it thoughtfully throughout the week. Use the list of daily readings to guide your Scripture reading for the rest of the week, and be sure to read the next Sunday Scripture before Mass so you'll get more out of the homily.

Reflections

- 💜 *What is your favorite Mass prayer*

- 💜 *What is your favorite Mass hymn?*

- 💜 *Think about the best homily you've ever heard. What did it teach you about your life?*

A Prayer to Share

Dear God,

Sundays are wonderful days. I love going to Mass, spending time with my family and with you. Sundays are great!

Love,

Lizzie

CHAPTER THIRTEEN

In the Company of God

*Rejoice always, pray without ceasing,
give thanks in all circumstances;
for this is the will of God in Christ Jesus for you.*
Thessalonians 5:16–18

How do I stay positive all the time? This is the number one question I'm asked both in person and through e-mail. My carefully considered answer—the one thing that works for me—is that I put everything into God's hands.

Everyone knows me as Lizzie, the girl who is so brave and so strong and never has a negative thing to say. It's my career and calling to motivate others and show people how to love themselves and be confidant in who they are, and I do that by being positive.

But the truth is, some days everything seems to go wrong. One annoying thing after another leaves me feeling frustrated and impatient. I still lose confidence in myself and let others define me. I still have days where I feel like giving up and staying in bed, days where finding the good in the bad doesn't come easily.

No matter how careful we are, we *all* have days like this.

For me, the antidote is the one who understands exactly what it's like to hide real pain behind a smile: God.

Put Yourself in God's Hands

When I was younger, praying was fun. It was something I did with my parents and at church. But as I got older, I also got lazy. For a while I prayed only before a test or when I was in trouble.

My relationship with God and prayer was like a rollercoaster. I'd pray really, really hard for some outcome, and then God wouldn't hear from me until I had another need. When God didn't give me the answers I was looking for, I'd get angry with him. When I got what I prayed for, I hardly noticed and never thanked him.

Once I starting accepting myself, I was able to be on better terms with God, to fully understand his love for me, and to pray, "Your will be done." I was able to relax and truly turn to prayer.

In the beginning, my requests were simple. I had much to be thankful for, and I knew I needed help, so I started with two simple sentences every day, all day. These words were my prayers. I started with the Sign of the Cross, said these two prayers, and crossed myself again:

Lord, help me.
Lord, thank you.

Over time I added the Our Father, a prayer I've known since childhood. I say the words slowly and think about what I'm saying.

Eventually I bought a journal and began to write my own prayers. The process of writing what is in my heart and the words I want to say to Jesus is truly a wonderful experience. I title and date each one. Capturing these personal prayers has helped me focus on my gifts and talents and to be thankful for them.

Gradually my book of prayers became full. I still have it and use it often.

How to Get Started

Writing your private conversations with God has many benefits. For one thing, having a written record of your faith journey makes it easier to chart your progress.

Find a journal or notebook you like so much that you can't wait to write in it, and then just start. If you're like me, some days the words will flow out of you, and on other days you'll struggle to get started. But if you're patient, the words will come. They may not be the greatest words ever written, but that doesn't matter. The important thing is to just start writing.

Here are some prompts to get you started:

Dear God, I am thankful for ….

Heavenly Father, I want to tell you…

At the end of this book are seven prayers I wrote for my morning conversations with God. Whenever you have trouble getting started, use one of those prayers. It doesn't matter that you didn't write it; what matters is that you're praying.

Reflections

💜 *What's your favorite formal prayer?*

💜 *Have you ever just let go of a problem and left it up to God? What did that feel like?*

💜 *The next time something is bothering you that is completely out of your control, how will you handle it?*

A Prayer to Share

Dear God,

I'm pretty sure you already know how much I cherish being able to talk to you about anything and everything, but I'm going to tell you again. I can talk to you without holding anything back because I know you'll love me no matter what I share, and that means everything to me. Thank you for your love, generosity, and forgiveness. I love you!

Love,

Lizzie

CHAPTER FOURTEEN

Find a Faith Model

Show yourself in all respects a model of good works,
and in your teaching show integrity, gravity.
Titus 2:7

One of my favorite saints is Saint Lucy. She was born in Sicily almost 300 years after the birth of Jesus. Of the many stories about her steadfast faith, here's the one that inspires me.

Lucy's family was very wealthy. When she grew up, she decided to become Christian, donate all her money and possessions to the poor, and stay single so she could devote her entire life to God.

Her mother had other ideas. In those days it was quite common for parents to arrange their children's marriages, and Lucy's mother had arranged one for her.

Lucy's mother had been sick for years, but she was cured after going on a religious pilgrimage. She was so grateful that she changed her mind about Lucy's marriage and gave a lot of the family money to the poor.

Lucy's intended bridegroom was very upset over losing Lucy and her money. It was illegal in Sicily to be Christian. To get even with her for jilting him, her ex-fiancé reported her to the authorities. They arrested her and condemned her to a life of prostitution. But when they tried to take her away, she stood as if cemented to the ground. Even the strongest guards couldn't move her, so the governor ordered them to build a fire around her. When the fire didn't kill her, they stabbed her to death.

Saint Lucy's astounding faith and courage helped her stay true to her decision to love God even in the midst of persecution. Her lesson for me: No matter what others say or do to try to lead you to a different path—no matter what the consequences are—it's right to stick to your beliefs.

But that's not the only reason Lucy is important to me. Her name means "light" in Latin, so she is the patron saint of people with eye problems.

Who Inspires You?

Quickly name three people (people you know or don't know, alive or dead) whose lives you find inspiring. If one or both of your parents come to mind, that's cool—but then you get to choose five people.

Write their names and the characteristics that make you most want to follow in their footsteps.

Next, think about your choices:
Do you admire these people for different reasons, or do they all have the same admirable qualities?

What do you have in common with them? Which of their qualities do you wish you had?

If each person has different admirable qualities, do they have other qualities—like gender, age, income, profession, race, location, anything—in common?

What do your choices tell you about yourself?

Why the Saints Are Important

In the Catholic Church, a saint is a dead person who has been officially declared by the Church to be in heaven and to be worthy of our admiration. Catholics don't worship saints—we see them as models for our own lives.

Many people think only perfect people are eligible for sainthood, but that's not true. Most of the saints were far from perfect when they lived on Earth; in other words, they were just like us. Even though they're dead—some for a very long time—they live on as examples. They had unique and beautiful lives, although many wouldn't have won any popularity contests.

Some Catholics view saints as faith-journey companions; others as patrons watching out for them. Either way, the saints show us how their love of God helped them overcome trouble and made their lives better.

Whenever I think about Saint Lucy, I'm inspired to follow my own path regardless of what others have to say about my prayerful decisions. Lucy's courage and strength in the face of danger is a testament to her undying faith. We share a place in God's community, and I'm grateful to know her story.

If you don't have a favorite saint, look online or at the library for saint stories. You're bound to find someone who interests you and whose life you find inspiring. Having that saint with you on your faith journey will add another dimension to your spiritual life.

Everyday Faith Models

I've been blessed to have many opportunities to share my story with many audiences. I've been asked which is my favorite, but how can I pick between elementary schools, with the sweetest and funniest kids, or leadership conferences, with eager young people ready to shine their light to help others?

Throughout each hour-long presentation, you can usually hear a pin drop because everyone is so focused on what I'm saying. I always leave time at the end for questions, which range from simple (what's my favorite color) to deep (how I pulled through all the negativity). I quickly realized after my first couple of speeches that even if someone doesn't have my syndrome, we share a bond of heartache and struggle.

During the meet-and-greets after my presentations, I hear individual stories of struggle. It's one of my favorite parts of speaking, because this is when I connect with my audience on a more personal level.

One meet-and-greet in particular has stayed with me. A fourth-grade teacher pulled me aside for a picture with her class of fifteen students. They were all eager to meet me and hug me and talk with me. While we were chatting, one of the girls teared up as she said other kids tease her about her ears. My heart broke for her. That can be traumatic for anyone, even more so for someone her age. I was so proud of her for speaking up even though it was so painful.

As we talked, her class was listening. Other students said they'd been teased too. It brought a tear to my eye when they assured the girl they'd stick up for her if it happened again.

Just like the weather, our lives have seasons. That little girl was

going through a stormy season, but with the help of her classmates and friends, she'll have brighter days ahead.

No matter our age or our circumstances, our lives are constantly under construction. As long as you have a strong foundation, you can build your life as high as you want to.

Reflections

💜 *Who is your favorite heavenly saint?*

💜 *Who is your favorite earthly saint?*

💜 *Who is in your personal community of saints here on Earth?*

A Prayer to Share

Dear God,

The biggest message I get from reading and knowing about the saints is just how much they trusted you. Their stories are great reminders for me.

Love,

Lizzie

CHAPTER FIFTEEN

Be Beautiful, Be You

The LORD is near to all who call on him,
to all who call on him in truth.
Psalm 145:18

After receiving the sacraments and completing my religious-education classes (Sunday School), I decided to become a religion teacher. I taught second-grade religion for three years with two of my best friends. Coming up with lesson plans and watching the kids learn about the love of God helped my faith grow stronger. It was also a lot of fun.

I loved the opening and closing prayers. We stood in a circle holding hands, and we started and ended with the Sign of the Cross. Before class, we prayed the Our Father; after class we prayed the Hail Mary. Praying as a class was very special for all of us.

I felt blessed that God gave me the opportunity to teach these kids and to worship together in his name. I'm thankful for the insights and graces that I received being part of this ministry. They taught me so much.

With each new class, we emphasized the importance of praying. We made sure our young students understood that they could pray in good times and bad and that they needed to pray all the time, not just when their brother or sister was about to tattle on them. We told them praying to God was like talking to a friend—a really good friend who wanted to hear from them. We taught them they can pray and talk to God during recess and thank him for a good day, and they can even thank him for pizza day in the cafeteria. That one always made them laugh.

It All Comes Back to Prayer

No matter how old you are, you'll find the power of prayer to be life-changing. This realization hit me at a confirmation retreat. I was a youth leader, and everyone was reflecting on their blessings. I remember being shocked at how much has happened in my life because of prayer. People I've never met pray for my health and recovery. Prayer has helped me get through days when I didn't want to get out of bed—days I felt overworked, stressed, tired, and annoyed with everything.

One afternoon when I was really feeling stressed, my mom suggested I go to my room and turn my cell phone off, put away my laptop, and lie down.

The idea sounded pretty horrible. When I'm without my cell phone, it's as though I'm disconnected from the world. I was sure I was going to fall asleep. At the very least, it was going to be a waste of time.

I spent the first half hour thinking about all the things I should have been doing, all the things I needed to get done. It took a while to change my thoughts from work and begin to focus on what was stressing me out. Soon I started crying.

Sometimes a good cry releases the tension that has been building up inside you. I started praying and asking God to help me. I continued to sit in silence and listen to what God was telling me. I took a bunch of deep breaths in and out and started telling myself I could do this. I needed to tackle one thing at a time and take baby steps.

I had been so focused on my appearance and on what others thought about me that I had been blind to the bigger picture. Because I was so upset with God, I didn't pray and ask for his help and encouragement to pull through.

Sometimes I still feel like I need to be Superwoman and help everyone who needs me, or I exhaust myself physically and emotionally trying to fix every problem I have. But I've learned that when I reach my limit, the best thing I can do is let go and let God. The best thing I can do is place my trust in him and to love him above all things.

It's amazing to see the power of faith, prayer, and God's love in my everyday life. Being a full-time college student, a motivational speaker, and an author are all huge blessings, but they keep my plate very full. Even though I love every minute of it, juggling all of it is hectic and draining.

The craziness usually comes in waves. Things slow down for a while, and I'm able to focus on school and keep up with my social life. But when I'm asked to give interviews and speeches, I sometimes feel like I can't catch my breath. I get sick very easily. Pretty much, if you have a cold, I'll pick it up. This is something I have no power over. I wash my hands all the time, but I can still get sick.

When that happens, instead of making myself feel worse with negative thoughts, I let God put his hands over me and help me get well again. I climb into bed and wait for my health to be restored.

We all need to open our hearts and minds to God's love—to lift up our worries, pain, sorrow, joy, and happiness to him and know that he's listening.

What's Your Next Move?

Now you know my story. I've shared my worst moments and how I was able to rise above them with God's help, and I've given you some tools to do the same thing in your life—with God's help.

We're all born with our own differences—characteristics that set us apart from everyone else. God made each of us in a specific way. He didn't make carbon copies. You were born with a purpose and the ability to set yourself apart from everyone else. *You are unique.*

I hope with all my heart that this book has convinced you that if you prayerfully love and trust God and pay attention to your passions, you'll become the person God wants you to be.

Don't settle for a mediocre life. Be beautiful! Be you!

Reflections

- 💜 *You are love!*

- 💜 *You are beautiful!*

- 💜 *You have much to be grateful for!*

- 💜 *If you wrote a book about your life, what would the title be?*

Seven Prayers to Share

I'll end this book with a prayer for each day of the week. Use them as a daily meditation or when you're having a hard time finding your own words. I pray for you every day, and I hope you'll pray for me.

Love,

Lizzie

𝓜onday PRAYER

. . . .

Dear Lord, please guide me through this week. Help me be strong when I feel weak, and help me cherish every moment of every day. When I feel hopeless, remind me of my blessings and help me remember you're always with me. Amen.

𝒯uesday PRAYER

. . . .

Dear Heavenly Father, grant me the will to stay focused on what I need to get done. Help me fight the temptation of giving in to gossip, social media, and whatever other distractions come my way. Keep my mind clear and open so I can accomplish my goals for the week. Amen.

Wednesday PRAYER

Dear Lord, thank you for granting me the blessings of strength, understanding, and will to accomplish the tasks that have been asked of me this week. I pray that you continue to encourage me on my journey throughout the rest of the week. Through you, I can accomplish all things. Amen.

Thursday PRAYER

Dear Heavenly Father, as the weekend approaches, please keep me mindful of what is right and wrong, and give me clarity as I make decisions. I look forward to the upcoming days of rest and relaxation. I pray for the safety of my loved ones, that they will be protected by your loving hands throughout the weekend. Amen.

𝓕𝓻𝓲𝓭𝓪𝔂 PRAYER

Dear Heavenly Father, thank you for your continued guidance, love, and encouragement throughout this week. I am also grateful for your forgiveness and understanding of my wrongdoings, doubtful thoughts, and negative actions. I'm thankful for the break I'll have from weekday stress and pressures. Amen.

𝓢𝓪𝓽𝓾𝓻𝓭𝓪𝔂 PRAYER

Dear Lord, grant me the focus to complete the tasks I put off during the week. Please allow me to concentrate on what I need to get done so I can fully enjoy time with my loved ones. Remind us of the love we have for one another, and help us never take our blessings for granted. I ask this through Christ our Lord. Amen.

Sunday Prayer

Dear Lord, thank you for the past week's highs and lows. I appreciate the good and the bad moments, and I'll take a lesson from each. Please show me how I can improve to make next week even better than the last. Amen.

Lizzie Velasquez, one of only three known people in the world with a
medical syndrome that doesn't allow her to gain weight or create muscle,
has appeared as a motivational speaker at more than 200 workshops.
Her story has been featured in both national and international media,
including the *Today Show, Inside Edition,* Australia's *Sunday Night,*
Germany's *Explosiv, Entertainment Tonight, The Doctors,* and *Dr. Drew.*
She has a bachelor's degree in communications from Texas State
University in San Marcos. This is her second book.